Andrés Guardado

To the Top!

2011 Guardado and Mexico win the Gold Cup championship. Guardado goes down to the Spanish Second Division with Deportivo la Coruña.

2010 He plays in his second World Cup.

2008 On November 27, he makes his first goal in the European League.

2007 On September 16, he makes his first official goal in the Spanish League. He makes his debut in both the Gold Cup and the America Cup.

2006 He plays his first World Cup in Argentina against Germany.

2005 He starts playing in the First Division with the Atlas.

1993 He enters the Atlas Soccer Club.

1986 September 28, José Andrés Guardado Hernández is born in Guadalajara, Jalisco.

Mason Crest
370 Reed Road
Broomall, Pennsylvania 19008
www.masoncrest.com

Printed and bound in the United States of America.

First printing
9 8 7 6 5 4 3 2 1

Series ISBN: 978-1-4222-2647-6
ISBN: 978-1-4222-2666-7
ebook ISBN: 978-1-4222-9207-5

Library of Congress Cataloging-in-Publication Data

Arturo Miranda Bravo, Jorge.
  Andres Guardado / by Jorge Arturo Miranda Bravo.
    p. cm.
  ISBN 978-1-4222-2666-7 (hardcover) – ISBN 978-1-4222-2647-6 (series hardcover) – ISBN 978-1-4222-9207-5 (ebook)
  1. Guardado, Andres, 1986–Juvenile literature. 2. Soccer players–Mexico–Biography–Juvenile literature. I. Title.
  GV942.7.G82A77 2013
  796.334092–dc23
  [B]
                                    2012031767

ABOUT THE AUTHOR:
JORGE ARTURO MIRANDA BRAVO was born in Mexico City, also known as "soccer city." Being far more talented with his hands and speech than with his feet and a soccer ball, Jorge pursued the path of journalism. He's worked for different radio stations including IMER (Mexican Radio Institute) and RADIORAMA, as well as independent stations in Mexico and the United States. Jorge also worked with David Faitelson on a sports broadcast popular in the southeastern United States, and has written for several sport magazines and newspapers as a journalist and reporter.

PICTURE CREDITS:
EFE Photos: 1, 4, 7, 8, 10, 11, 13, 14, 17, 18, 21, 22, 23, 24, 26, 27, 28, 29
Dreamstime.com: 12

SUPERSTARS OF SOCCER
Andrés Guardado

CONTENTS

Andrés Guardado, the "Little Prince" of Guadalajara, is a young player with a short but successful career.

CHAPTER 1

A Powerful Talent

Soccer fans know why they love the game. They love seeing a player totally in control of the ball. It almost seems glued to his feet! Fans love watching players on the other team get left behind.

Watching any good soccer player is exciting. But watching a player with a strong left leg can be even more amazing. Most soccer players mainly use their right leg to control the ball. Not many players use their left leg. Players who use their left leg can pull off surprising moves fans and other players don't expect. Andrés Guardado is one of these players.

THE MIDGET

José Andrés Guardado Hernández was born on September 28, 1986. He was born in Guadalajara, Mexico. His parents were Teresa Hernández and Andrés Manuel Guardado. Andrés grew up with two older brothers who called him "the Midget." Even today, at his full height, he's shorter than a lot of players.

Andrés looked like he was going to be a soccer star right from the start. He liked to kick things around. His father would toss balloons at him, and Andrés would naturally kick them back rather than use his hands. He always used his left foot.

For a little while, the young Guardado would try to play soccer in his family's house. He ended up breaking a lot of things! Then his brothers introduced him to children's teams he could play on.

Right away, he proved that he was good at soccer. He could play better than kids who were older than him.

NEXT STEPS

The children's team that Guardado was playing for was soon too easy. He needed more of a challenge. When he was just seven, he started playing at an **ACADEMY** run by Club Atlas in Guadalajara. His coach was Virginia Tovar, the first woman to ever coach in Mexican soccer.

Guardado was very young to be playing such serious soccer. He wasn't really prepared for this new life. There were lots of changes, and he didn't deal with them well at first. Guardado started rebelling and getting in trouble. His behavior got in the way of playing, too, and he had to sit out a lot.

When he was fourteen, Guardado decided to take a break from soccer. He dropped out of his club. He wasn't sure how long he'd stay away from the sport.

Guardado's older brother Manuel Alejandro helped him get back on his feet. He knew his younger brother really did want to play soccer and just needed another chance.

Manuel Alejandro was playing **PROFESSIONALLY** for the Athletic Club of Cihuatlan. He talked to his coach and got Andrés a spot on the team. Guardado started playing in the Second Division.

While playing with his new team, Guardado learned to love soccer again. He also changed positions on the field. Guardado began playing **MIDFIELD** rather than left wing. Soon, he was one of the team's best players.

BACK AND FORTH

An important coach, Sergio Bueno, started to notice Guardado. Bueno invited the young star to train with him. He wanted to get Guardado into a top team in Mexico, in the First Division.

Training for the best division in Mexican soccer was hard. Guarda-do was closer to playing with the pro league than ever before. But all the changes in his life were too much for the young player. He wasn't playing as well as he knew he could. Soon, Guardado was sent back to the youth division. He was going through a tough time, but it wouldn't be long before he found his way again.

Guardado's old team, Club Atlas, knew that he was a great soccer player. They knew he just needed another chance. The team soon hired Guardado back. Even better, they hired him to be on their First Division team.

PRO PLAYER

Finally, on August 20, 2005, Guardado had his chance. His first game was during the Apertura (championship) games. Club Atlas played against Club Pachuca. Guardado's team went on to win the game. What a way to start a career!

Two months later, in October, Guardado got his first goal in the First Division. Atlas was playing the Tigers. Guardado was showing Mexico that he really was a star.

Guardado's playing caught the attention of lots of people. Experts, journalists, and fans all started to keep an eye on him. They began calling Guardado "the Silver Fox."

About a year after his first game, Guardado earned a place in fans' hearts. He scored two great goals against a rival team, América. Only a gifted player could have scored the same goals. After

An Atlas fan gets Guardado's autograph.

Lefties on the Field

Approximately 13 percent of the world's population uses their left side more than their right. In the past, people who were left-handed were made fun of, or even feared. Sometimes teachers and other people forced lefties to use their right hands. Left-sided soccer players don't have to worry about that anymore, though. Now, players who use their left leg can have an edge over right-legged players. Some of the greatest soccer players from Mexico have powerful left legs. They include Diego Armando Maradona, Ramón Ramírez, Ramón Morales, and Hugo Sánchez.

the game, fans gave Guardado another nickname—"El principito," the "Little Prince."

Guardado has played at many different levels in Mexican soccer.

CHAPTER 2

Prince of the World Cup

Nobody could miss the Little Prince when he stepped on the field. Guardado seemed to glide across left field. He left his opponents stunned. Guardado was a quick player, but he was also known for thinking quickly on the field.

MAKING NATIONAL

So far, Guardado had been playing at the highest level of Mexican league soccer. But there was one more level above that—the Mexican national team.

The national team's coach invited Guardado to play a little with them. The coach was called the "Great Fox." The Great Fox and the Silver Fox were coming together.

In just four months, Guardado went from starting out in the First Division to playing on the national team. Many soccer players can only dream of what Guardado had done.

The first game Guardado played with the national team was in the United States. It was a **FRIENDLY MATCH** between Mexico and Hungary. The game was the last of the year. Guardado came out on the field as a **SUBSTITUTE** for another player.

Guradado impressed his coach. The Great Fox even started to think about including the young player on the national team. But nothing was for sure yet.

PASSPORT TO GERMANY

In 2006, Guardado had a chance to play for Mexico in the World Cup. Lots of other good soccer players wanted the same chance, though. They wanted to play for their country, too. Guardado had to wait and find out if he made it on the national team for the World Cup in Germany.

Finally, the coach told the players who he had chosen. He said, "As far as **LATERAL** defenders and lateral midfielders are concerned: Castro, Mendez, Osorio, "Maza" Rodriguez, "Rafa" Marquez, Suarez, Huiqui, Salcido… Guardado." Guardado's family and friends couldn't have been happier. His

name was listed with some of the greatest players in Mexico.

Guardado kept calm. This was just the first round. There were more names on the list than people who could actually play in the World Cup. Three names wouldn't make it to the final list.

Guardado knew he had to play his best. He had to impress the coach. Lots of things could happen. He could get injured. He could start playing badly. Or everyone else could just play better.

There was no need to worry. Guardado kept up his amazing playing. In the end, he was invited onto the national team. He was going to the World Cup!

Just because he was on the team, though, didn't mean he got to play in every game. Mexico's first World Cup game was against Iran. Guardado had to sit on the bench for this one. He celebrated with his team as Mexico won 3–1.

He sat out the next two games, too. Mexico went 0–0 with Angola and lost 2–1 against Portugal. Guardado was getting angry. He wanted to play and

Guardado moves past Gonzalo Jara of Chile in a friendly match before the South African World Cup.

Guardado keeps the ball away from yet another player.

The young player became a star with the Deportivo of la Coruña!

The Mexican team poses for a photo in the World Cup 2010. From left to right and top to bottom, the players are: Oscar Pérez, Ricardo Osorio, Rafael Márquez, Francisco Rodríguez, Gerardo Torrado, Adolfo Bautista, Efraín Juárez, Andrés Guardado, Carlos Salcido, Giovani Dos Santos, and Javier Hernández.

help his team win. He thought he wouldn't get to play in the World Cup after all.

Finally, he got his chance. In the next game against Argentina, the coach put him on the field. He told Guardado, "Get out there and make them respect you."

Guardado played for a little more than an hour. Argentina ended up winning because of a great goal, but Guardado had gotten to play. He was so young, but he had already played in the World Cup.

The Great Fox

Ricardo La Volpe is known as the Great Fox. He was born in Argentina, but has worked with soccer teams in many different countries. He first played on the Argentinian team that won the World Cup, and later went on to coach the Mexican national team (where he met Andrés Guardado). Later, he worked in Costa Rica. La Volpe can sometimes have a short temper, but he's a great coach!

Guardado became a star player on the Mexican national team.

CHAPTER 3

A Fox Dressed in Green

Everything seemed to move very fast for Andrés Guardado. He kept playing in the green uniform of the national team. And he kept proving that he deserved to play with Mexico's best. In 2007, he scored his first goal for the national team in a game against Venezuela. Guardado was at the top of his game, and only getting better.

UPS AND DOWNS WITH MEXICO

Guardado was playing all over the world. In 2007, he played in the Gold Cup in the United States. The Gold Cup is a regional championship for CON-CACAF (Confederation of North, Central American, and Caribbean Association Football).

Mexico won a few games, but they weren't playing very well. Then, the Mexican team lost to Honduras. Although Mexico made it to the finals, the team's chances at winning weren't looking very good.

In the finals, Mexico played the United States, its biggest **RIVAL** in the Gold Cup. Guardado scored his first goal with the national team during the game. Even with Guardado's big goal, Mexico eventually lost the game.

The Mexican national team had another chance to prove itself in the 2007 America Cup. The America Cup is a championship played in South America. Two teams from outside the area are also invited to play. Mexico is often invited to play in the America Cup.

Guardado was hurt, so he didn't play in the first two games of the Cup. Soon, though, he got back in the game. With Guardado playing, Mexico tied a game, won one against Paraguay, and then faced Argentina again. Argentina was the team they couldn't beat. Mexico lost to Argentina again.

Mexico still had a chance to win third place in the Cup. This time, Guardado stepped up. He scored a goal against Uruguay. His goal meant that Mexico won third place!

SOUTH AFRICA 2010

Not every great player has been able to play in a World Cup. But Andrés Guardado has played in two.

The Gold Cup

The Gold Cup is a contest between soccer teams from North America, Central America, the Caribbean, and a couple of South American countries. It is held every two years. Every other Gold Cup also leads to the World Cup. The top three teams in the Gold Cup get to go to the World Cup. Mexico and the United States have won the most Gold Cups in recent years.

Four years after his World Cup debut, Guardado was back. It was his second Cup, and he was just twenty-four. This time he was playing for Mexico in South Africa.

Mexico played against South Africa in the very first game of the Cup. Eighty-four thousand people were watching. There was a lot of pressure on both teams!

Guardado didn't start the game, but he entered after about an hour. Just a few minutes later, he got an **ASSIST**, and Mexico made a goal. Mexico ended up tying South Africa.

Mexico went on to win the next game, although Guardado didn't play.

The team lost the next match to Uruguay.

However, Mexico made it to the next round of playing. They now had to play Argentina, just like they had at the last World Cup. Mexicans everywhere remembered how the team had lost. They hoped that this year would be different.

This time, Guardado was a **STARTER**. But, sadly for Mexico, the team lost to Argentina again, 3–1. The World Cup was over for Mexico. Guardado had gotten a lot of playing time, though. He was truly a star in his home country.

2011 GOLD CUP

2011 was another Gold Cup year. Mexico wanted it to be a better one than 2007. Once again, Andrés Guardado was invited to be part of the national team.

First, Mexico played against teams that weren't as good. They won against El Salvador and Cuba. Then, they faced Costa Rica. The coach for Costa Rica was the Great Fox, the coach that had originally invited Guardado to the Mexican national team.

Guardado didn't let that bother him. He focused on winning, no matter who was on the other side. In fact, he scored a great goal, leading Mexico to a 4–1 win.

Mexico was doing well in this Gold Cup. They went to the next round, and won against Guatemala. Guardado

Guardado keeps the ball away from Paraguayan player Darío Verón.

played in the entire game. He didn't have to worry about getting on the field. Now he was one of the biggest stars!

Mexico kept on winning. They won the semifinals and ended up in the final championship game. If they won this game, Mexico would get to play in the 2013 Confederations Cup against teams from all over the world.

The final game was against the United States. At first, the United States was winning. Then Mexico started fighting back on the field. The Little Prince tied the game 2–2. He even helped make the next goal. Guardado and his team won the finals, 4–2! The Mexican national team had turned their game around.

Mexico was going to the Confederations Cup in Brazil in 2013. Guardado hoped to be part of his hometeam when the time came. Maybe he could lead them to a championship!

Fans around the world got used to seeing Andrés Guardado on the field.

 CHAPTER 4

The New Galician

Guardado became successful very quickly. He became a national player soon after he started playing professionally. First Mexicans were watching him. Then the world was.

After the 2006 German World Cup, all the experts agreed. Andrés Guardado wouldn't stay in Mexico forever. He would play for some of the best teams in the world.

There were many rumors about different teams Guardado might join. None of the rumors were true, though. Guardado kept playing for Mexico for three seasons.

In July 2007, the Little Prince made a big change. The president of the Club Atlas announced that Guardado was signing to the Deportivo Club of la Coruña in Spain. Coruña is in Galicia, in northern Spain.

MOVING ON

On July 18, Guardado played his last game at home. The Little Prince only played for fifteen minutes. With tears in his eyes, Guardado said goodbye. He said, "I want to tell the people, the faithful, the fans: thank you; I will forever be red and black." (Red and black are Mexico's colors when they play internationally.) Guardado's new colors were blue and white. He would be playing in a new stadium and a new country.

Meanwhile, fans of Deportivo were very happy to have the Mexican star. They gave him a big welcome to his new team. Guardado said, "It's a huge responsibility to be seen that way by the people, because they expect a lot from you."

Guardado had almost always worn number seventeen on his uniform. He always wanted to wear eighteen, though. He had worn the number when he played at the Germany World Cup. He asked Deportivo for eighteen. He wanted a new start with his new team.

Deportivo needed some help. They had finished thirteenth the year before. Maybe Guardado was the player they needed to turn things around.

Guardado started training right away. He felt at home with the team. And the team accepted him too.

Playing for Different Countries

Soccer players can actually play for different countries. Andrés Guardado has played for both Mexican and Spanish league teams. Teams are free to sign players from any country. However, only certain people **QUALIFY** to play on national teams. Players have to be citizens of the country they play for. So Guardado only qualifies to play on Mexico's national team in international competitions like the World Cup.

New and Old Galicias

Mexico was taken over by the Spanish during the 1500s. One of the Spanish conquerers was named Nuño Beltrán de Guzmán. He traveled to Mexico from Spain and conquered the area around what is now Guadalajara. He called his new land "the New Kingdom of Galicia." So, Guardado was born in New Galicia. Now he was making his way to old Galicia.

GREAT START

Guardado got used to his new team quickly. In August 2007, he played his first game wearing blue and white. It was a big game. Deportivo was playing Real Madrid, one of the best teams in the country.

With Guardado, Deportivo won! They beat Real Madrid 2–1. It was a great start with his new team.

A month later, the Little Prince scored his first official goal in the Spanish League. It was an impressive goal, and fans knew that their team had made a good choice when it signed Guardado.

A new era began for Deportivo. Having Guardado on the team was everything the coach had hoped for. He said, "Let no one forget that he is a great player. He is an amazing addition, and I am very excited for next year, and have to take care of him, because I'm sure he will be a huge star. Next year is Andrés' year, no doubt."

By the end of the season, Deportivo was doing a lot better. They finished in ninth place and had scored more goals. Guardado himself had scored five goals.

HAPPY TIMES

The next season was another good one for Guardado. His team was in ninth place again, and fought for the top spots in the Spanish League. He scored two goals and assisted in eight more.

Guardado also got to play in European tournaments. It was something he had wanted to do ever since he was little. His dreams came true as he scored a goal against Holland.

On July 23, 2007 Guardado left Atlas and started playing for Deportivo.

The next season was just the same. He played in twenty-three games. He made three goals and assisted with five. Guardado also scored the first goal in the King's Cup (the Spanish championship game).

CORUÑA FALLS

During the 2010–2011 season, things started to fall apart. Guardado suffered from some serious injuries. Most soccer players have to deal with an injury at one point or another.

Guardado wasn't able to play his best while hurt. He only played in nineteen games. Guardado sat out for half of the season to get better. Even though he didn't play as much as the year before, he still scored two goals and assisted one more.

Without Guardado, Deportivo got worse. They left the First Division in Spanish soccer. Now they were part of the Second Division, also called the Liga Adelante.

By May, Deportivo had won just ten games and lost sixteen. They were in eighteenth place, worse than they had been before Guardado started playing.

Guardado was also having other troubles. During the summer of 2011, his agent said that Guardado would

Guardado and
his Deportivo
teammates lift the
Teresa Herrera
trophy after
beating Real
Madrid 2–1.

stop playing for Deportivo because they were so bad. He said that Guardado didn't want to play in the Second Division.

Fans thought Guardado was abandoning his team. They wanted him to help get Deportivo back in shape. They didn't want him to leave when times were tough. Crowds started booing him on the field. In the pre-season, some crowds even sang hate songs.

LIGA ADELANTE

Guardado didn't let all that get him down. He decided the 2012 season would be his best yet. He decided he would get fans to like him again. His final goal was to move Deportivo back to the First Division. Guardado planned to prove everyone wrong.

In many countries, the Second Division is often overlooked. Fans often pay closer attention to the top teams. Club fans didn't think Guardado would pay much attention to the Second Division either. To their surprise, Andrés took the challenge. He stayed with the team and kept playing alongside his teammates.

Things soon started to look better for Deportivo. In the next season, Guardado was back to playing his best. Deportivo won thirteen games. Guardado himself had eight goals. He had some of the highest scores in the Liga Adelante. He didn't abandon his team, and he played very well.

The winter can be cold in South Africa, so Guardado and other players suit up for practice.

Guardado made waves with his playing in Spain.

CHAPTER 5

Andrés Today

Fans all over the world have good things to say about Andrés Guardado.

"Guardado has the speed and skill to win…that every major player must have," said team **MANAGER** Michael Laudrup after seeing the Silver Fox in action.

Guardado has done amazing things while playing in Spain. He scored eighteen goals with Deportivo. He played in the European League and the King's Cup. Guardado has proven his soccer skills to fans around the world.

HARD TIMES

Though Guardado has had a great career in soccer, things haven't been perfect for the sports star. Everyone has good times and bad. Gaurdado has had his share of troubles in his personal and professional life.

In December 2006, he married Briana Morales. At first, Guardado and his wife were happy. He played better during his first seasons with Deportivo partly because he was happy. But soon, Guardado's marriage began to fall apart. He and Briana got divorced in 2011.

Injuries have also gotten in Guardado's way. In February 2008, Guardado hurt his leg. He had to sit on the bench for six weeks. The injury kept bothering him in later games as well.

Later that year, Guardado injured the knee in his other leg. And in 2009, he was hurt yet again. He had to sit out for a month. Guardado's team lost some games because he couldn't play.

Since the 2010 World Cup, Guardado has had five more injuries. But the Little Prince doesn't let being hurt stop him. He keeps coming back, playing just as well as before.

THE NEXT MOVE

In early 2012, Guardado told fans that he would be leaving Deportivo. In May, he signed with a new team. Guardado decided to stay in Spain and play for Valencia.

Although he's still young, Guardado has been a major part of the teams he's played on.

It was another dream come true. Guardado was going to be playing for a great team. He had to learn new things and play even better.

"Now I will have tougher demands on me, a lot of competition and great players around me who are going to push me even harder than before," Guardado

Guardado stayed with Deportivo to help them move back up to the First Division.

Andrés has celebrated some big wins with teammates and fans over the years.

The Mexican player glides over the field in a game between Deportivo and Celta Vigo.

said. "Obvoiusly this will improve me as a player, which will in turn transfer over to my national team." The Little Prince is still ready to learn more about soccer and become a better player.

There's no slowing down for Andrés Guardado. He has a new team to play on and new things to learn. Between his time in Spain and his time playing for the Mexican national team, Guardado has many amazing things left to do. Fans will keep a close eye on the Mexican star in the years to come.

FIND OUT MORE
On the Internet

ESPN SOCCERNET GUARDADO PROFILE

soccernet.espn.go.com/player/_/id/76932/Andrés-guardado?cc=5901

ESPN.COM SOCCER NEWS

espn.go.com/sports/soccer

FIFA.COM MEXICO

www.fifa.com/associations/association=mex/index.html

FOOTRENDS.COM

uk.footrends.com/top/Andrés+guardado

GOAL.COM MEXICAN SOCCER NEWS

www.goal.com/en-us/news/114/mexico

GLOSSARY

ACADEMY: A place of study or training.

ASSIST: An action that helps another player score a goal.

FRIENDLY MATCH: A game that does not count as an official competition; the outcome doesn't have anything to do with the team's standing.

LATERAL: Having to do with the sides, rather than the center.

MANAGER: The person in charge of the training and strategy of a sports team.

MIDFIELD: Players in the middle of the field who help defend and attack when needed.

PROFESSIONALLY: Playing for money.

QUALIFY: To be eligible for.

RIVAL: Traditional competitor.

STARTER: Player who participates in the beginning of a game.

SUBSTITUTE: Something or someone serving in place of another.

INDEX